HOW TALL?

THOMSON
━━★━━
GALE

For more information, contact
The Gale Group, Inc.
27500 Drake Rd.
Farmington Hills, MI 48331-3535
Or you can visit our Internet site at http://www.gale.com

First published in 2003 by Orpheus Books Ltd., 2 Church Green, Witney, Oxfordshire, OX28 4AW

© 2003 Orpheus Books Ltd.

Created and produced by Nicholas Harris, Claire Aston, and Emma Godfrey, Orpheus Books Ltd.

Text: Nicholas Harris

Consultant: Dr. Charles Evans

Illustrators: Sebastian Quigley (Linden Artist), Ray Grinaway, and Mike Fuller

LIBRARY OF CONGRESS CATALOGING-IN-PUBLICATION DATA

Harris, Nicholas.
  How Tall? / by Nicholas Harris.
    p. cm. — (How?)
Includes bibliographical references and index.
Summary: Compares the height of many things.
  ISBN 1-41030-065-X (hardback : alk. paper) 1-41030-194-X (softcover : alk. paper)
  1.—Juvenile literature. 2. I. Title. II. Series.
QL49 .N5363 2004
590 21—dc21

Printed in Singapore
10 9 8 7 6 5 4 3 2 1

HOW TALL?

by Nicholas Harris

BLACKBIRCH™
PRESS

THOMSON
★
GALE

Detroit • New York • San Diego • San Francisco • Cleveland • New Haven, Conn. • Waterville, Maine • London • Munich

HOW TO USE THIS BOOK

For each double page, all the illustrations are drawn to scale. The tallest thing is featured again on the following double page, where it appears as the *shortest* thing. (You can find it quickly because its label is contained in a box.) The illustrations on this double page are also all drawn to scale and the tallest thing is again featured on the next double page. And so on, all the way through the book.

MEASUREMENTS

Where the metric equivalent is given, the conversion is approximate.

0.0003 in *means* three ten-thousandths of an inch

0.008 inches *means* eight thousandths of an inch.

0.01 inches *means* one hundredth of an inch.

0.1 inches *means* one tenth of an inch.

in *is an abbreviation of* inches

ft *is an abbreviation of* feet

mm *is an abbreviation of* millimeter.

cm *is an abbreviation of* centimeter.

m *is an abbreviation of* meter.

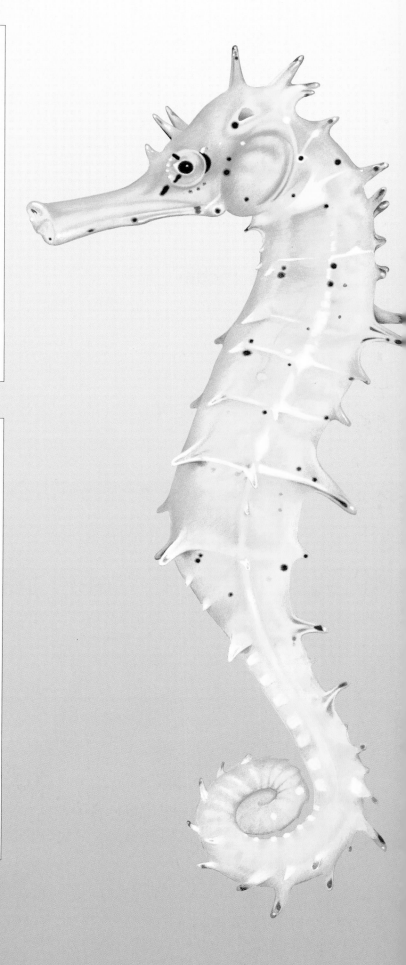

CONTENTS

0.012 in

0.01 in

0.008 in

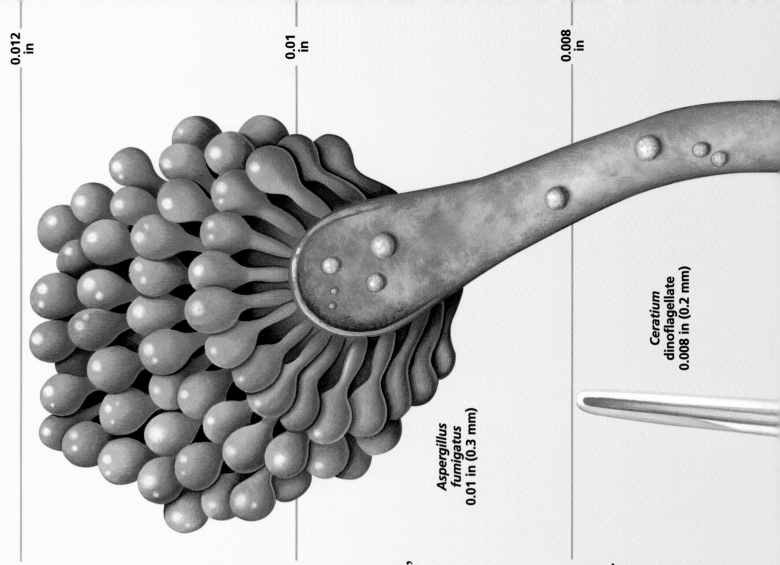

Aspergillus fumigatus
0.01 in (0.3 mm)

Ceratium
dinoflagellate
0.008 in (0.2 mm)

TO SEE anything on these pages in detail, you would need a microscope. A nanothermometer is an extremely tiny thermometer. It is used for measuring the temperature inside the bloodstream. It is one of a number of very tiny devices that are specially made to fit inside the human body.

The foot of a gecko, a kind of lizard, has millions of tiny hairs sticking out beneath it. Each hair, a tiny fraction of an inch high, has lots of sticky endings. These allow the gecko to walk up walls and upside down along ceilings—even if the surfaces are smooth and glassy.

Diatoms and dinoflagellates are microscopic, plant-like living things called algae. They live in ponds, rivers, and oceans. There are sometimes so many of them that they turn the water a green or red color. The horns of this dinoflagellate help it to float upright in the water.

The tallest thing on these pages is *Aspergillus fumigatus*. It is a kind of mold or fungus. Large numbers of *Aspergillus* grow on all kinds of things like dead leaves or animals. They also grow in the soil itself. If you are unlucky enough to breathe in some *Aspergillus*, they can make you sick.

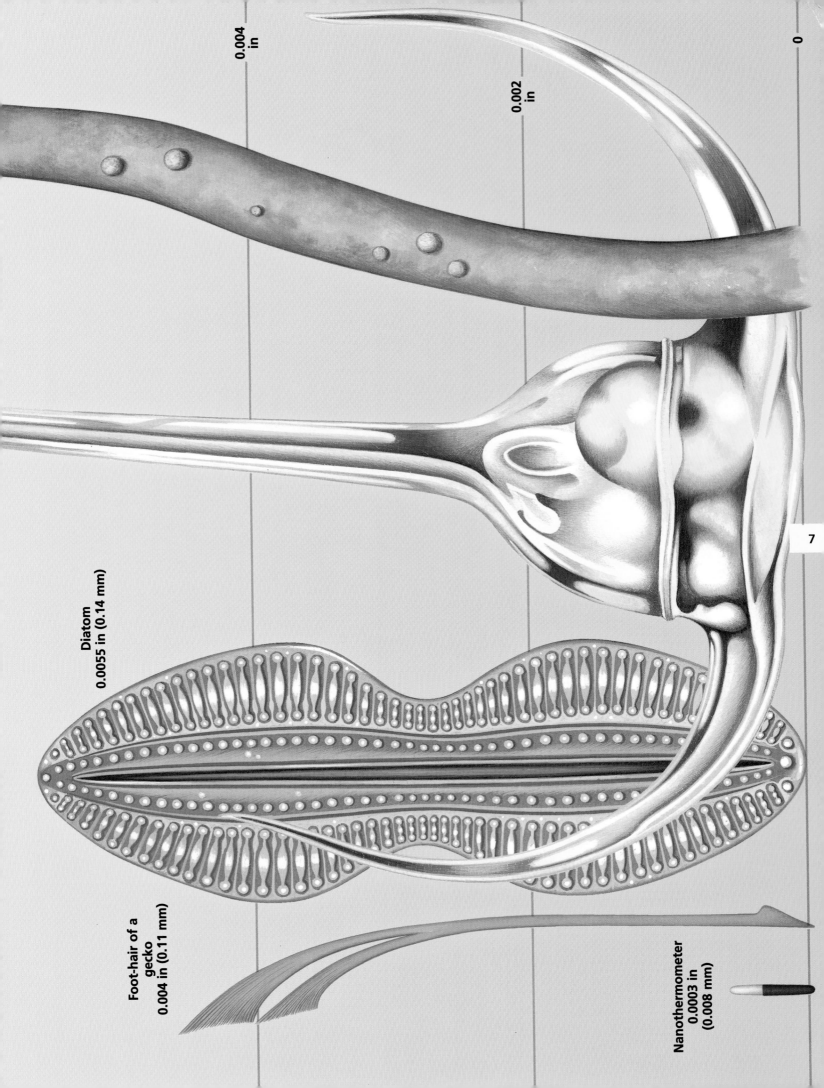

0.004
in

0.002
in

0

Diatom
0.0055 in (0.14 mm)

7

Foot-hair of a
gecko
0.004 in (0.11 mm)

Nanothermometer
0.0003 in
(0.008 mm)

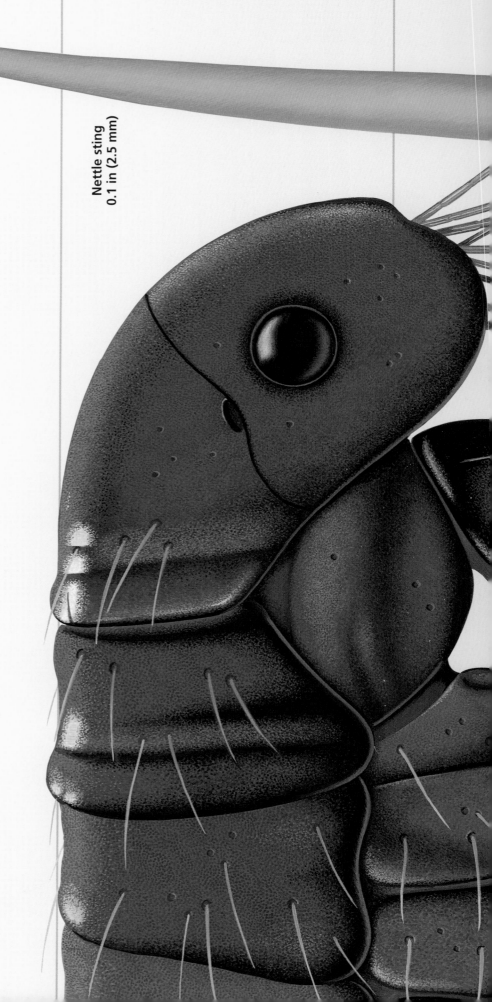

0.1 in

0.08 in

0.06 in

Nettle sting
0.1 in (2.5 mm)

COVERED in tiny bristles, fleas find it very easy to cling on to another animal while it runs, flies, or swims. A flea's body is flattened from side to side. It is the ideal shape for "swimming" through fur or feathers. Fleas can pierce their host's skin with their mouths and suck up the blood. And, to make a quick getaway, they can leap up to 150 times their own length. That's the same as a person jumping over the Eiffel Tower (*see page 22*)!

The rootless duckweed is the world's smallest plant. You could fit 25 of them across your fingernail! Masses of them float on the surface of streams and ponds.

Hairs grow on the undersides of nettle leaves. They contain chemicals that sting you when the pointed tip pierces your skin.

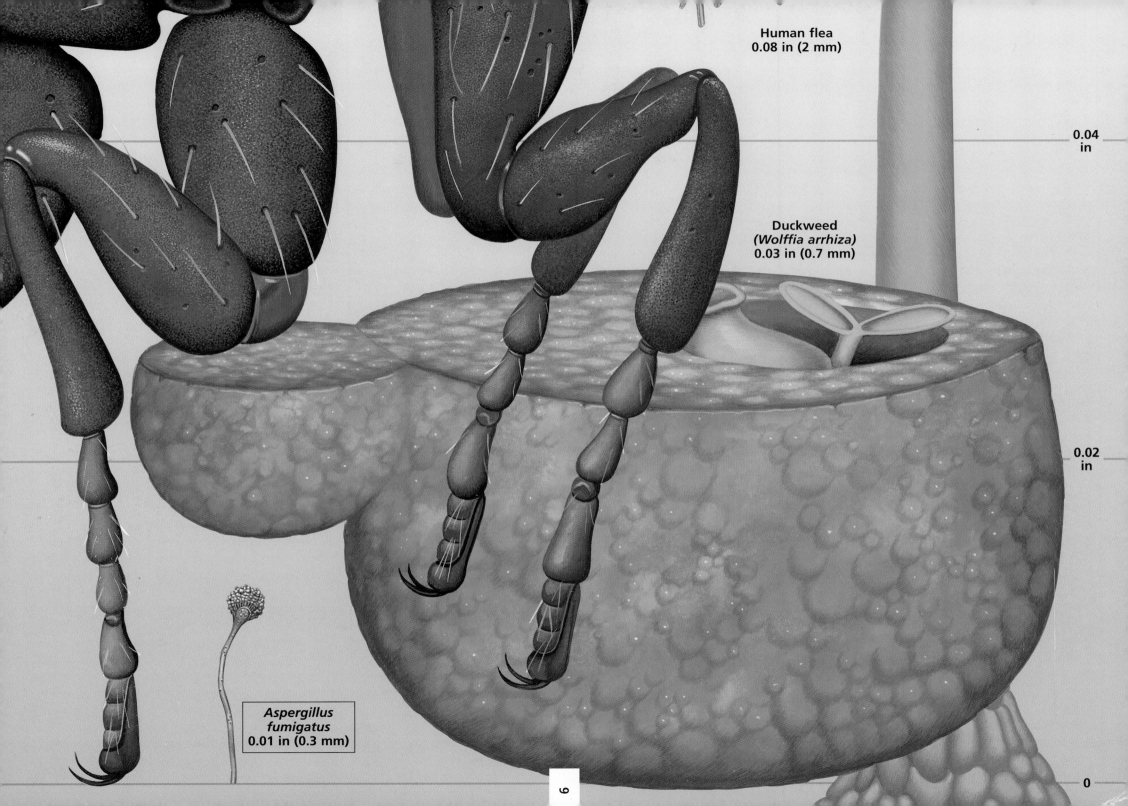

Human flea
0.08 in (2 mm)

0.04
in

Duckweed
(*Wolffia arrhiza*)
0.03 in (0.7 mm)

0.02
in

Aspergillus fumigatus
0.01 in (0.3 mm)

0

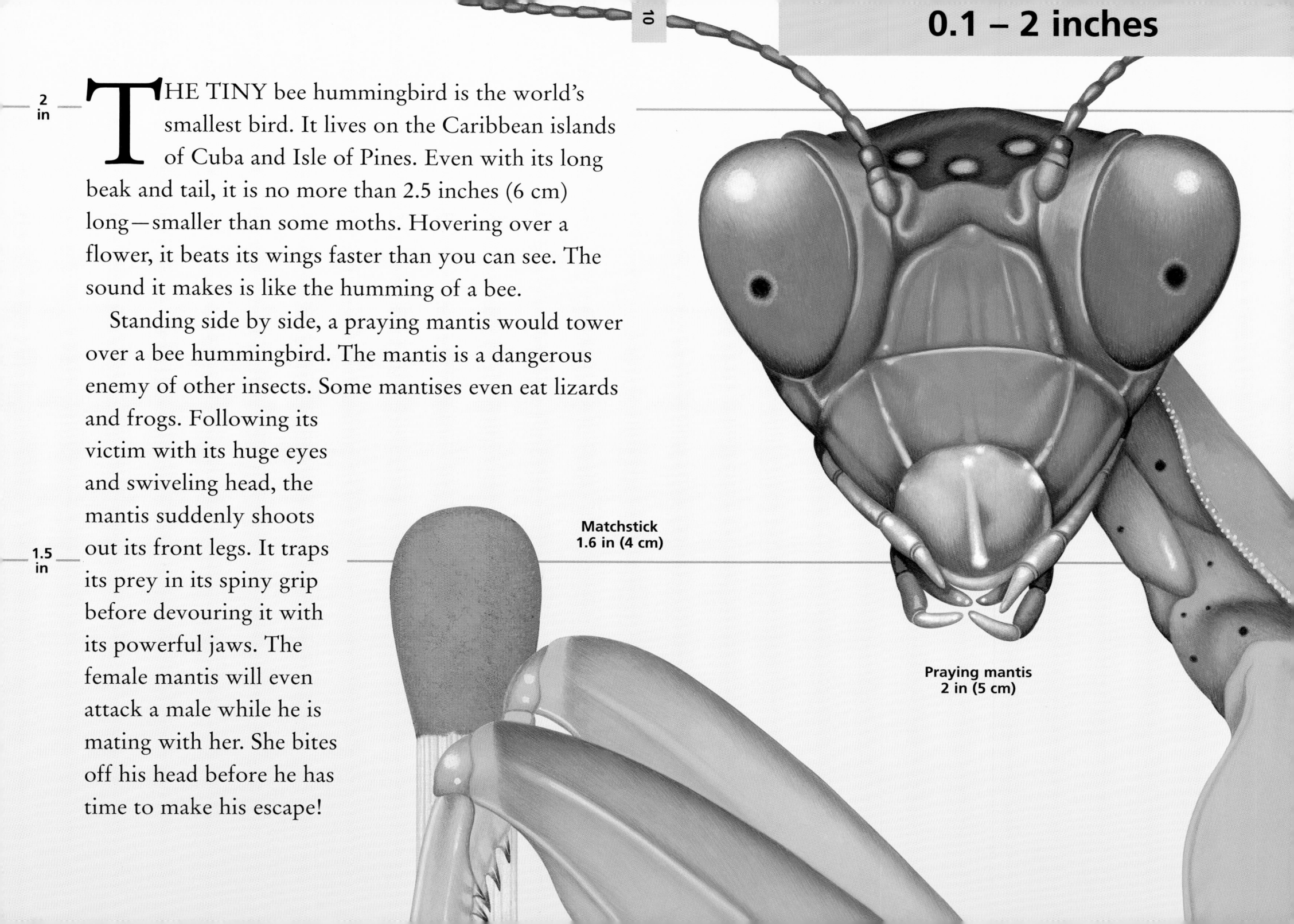

2 in

THE TINY bee hummingbird is the world's smallest bird. It lives on the Caribbean islands of Cuba and Isle of Pines. Even with its long beak and tail, it is no more than 2.5 inches (6 cm) long—smaller than some moths. Hovering over a flower, it beats its wings faster than you can see. The sound it makes is like the humming of a bee.

Standing side by side, a praying mantis would tower over a bee hummingbird. The mantis is a dangerous enemy of other insects. Some mantises even eat lizards and frogs. Following its victim with its huge eyes and swiveling head, the mantis suddenly shoots out its front legs. It traps its prey in its spiny grip before devouring it with its powerful jaws. The female mantis will even attack a male while he is mating with her. She bites off his head before he has time to make his escape!

1.5 in

Matchstick 1.6 in (4 cm)

Praying mantis 2 in (5 cm)

Cuban bee hummingbird
1 in (2.5 cm)

Before it is born, a baby is called an embryo in its very early stages. At four weeks old, a human embryo looks a lot like the embryo of a dog, chicken, or a fish! It even has a tail, although this shrinks away later. The head and the brain are the largest parts. It already has a heart.

0.5 in

Human embryo at 4 weeks
0.3 in (7 mm)

Nettle sting
0.1 in (2.5 mm)

0

THE LESSER MOUSE DEER is from the rain forests of Southeast Asia. It is the smallest hoofed animal in the world. It is 8 inches (20 cm) high at the shoulder, and weighs no more than 4.5 pounds (2 kg). Despite its tiny size, the male deer can be quite fierce when it needs to protect itself or its mate. It uses its tusks as weapons. But nothing can protect these tiny deer from large birds of prey or hungry crocodiles. So they come out only at night, when they scurry about in search of fallen fruit, fungi, and leaves on the forest floor.

The thorny seahorse is named for the long, sharp spines that cover its body. It lives near coral reefs in warm ocean waters. Like all seahorses, it moves slowly along in an upright position. It can grip onto sea plants using its curly tail. The female places the eggs she has laid in the male's special pouch.

8
in

6
in

**Lesser mouse deer
8 in (20 cm) at
the shoulder**

**Thorny seahorse
6 in (15 cm)**

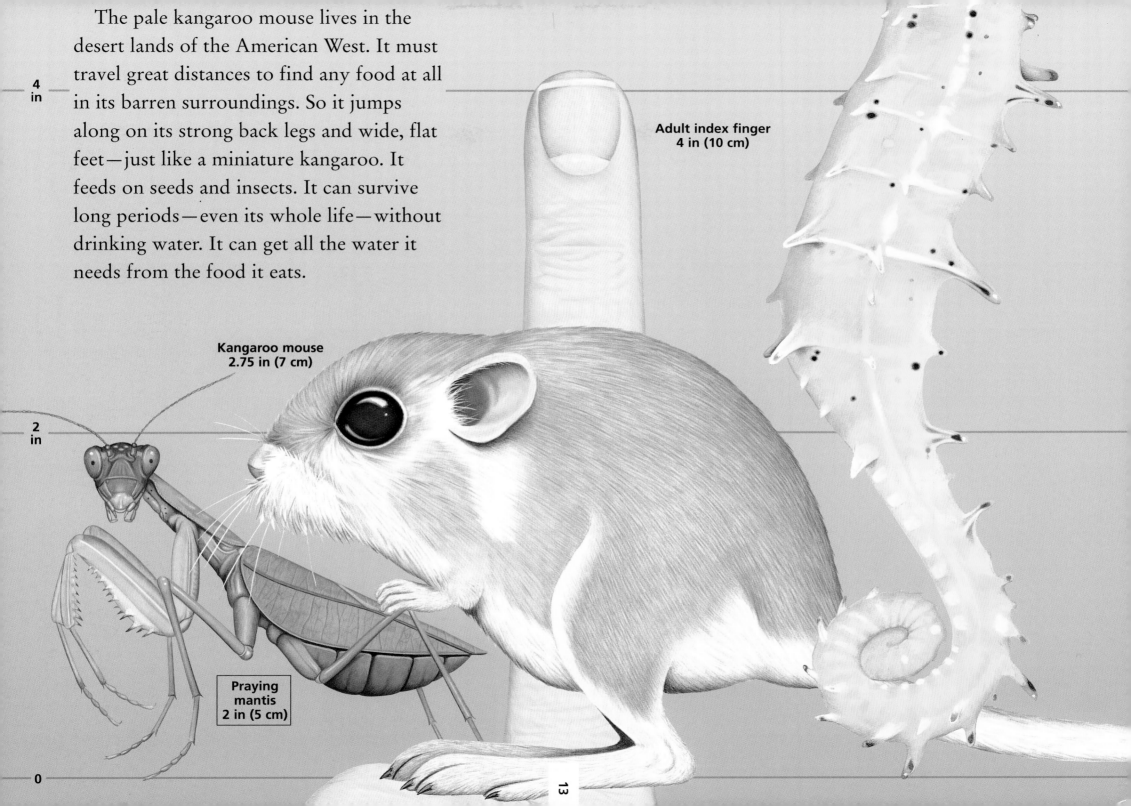

The pale kangaroo mouse lives in the desert lands of the American West. It must travel great distances to find any food at all in its barren surroundings. So it jumps along on its strong back legs and wide, flat feet—just like a miniature kangaroo. It feeds on seeds and insects. It can survive long periods—even its whole life—without drinking water. It can get all the water it needs from the food it eats.

4 in

**Adult index finger
4 in (10 cm)**

**Kangaroo mouse
2.75 in (7 cm)**

2 in

**Praying
mantis
2 in (5 cm)**

0

THE EMPEROR penguin is the tallest member of the penguin family. In the water, emperors swim fast and gracefully. On land, they can only waddle about clumsily. Luckily, they live on the ice around the coasts of Antarctica, so they can move around by sliding along over the ice on their bellies!

The male emperor penguin stands around much of the time. After mating, his female partner returns to the sea. She leaves her egg on his feet, where he keeps it warm under a flap of skin and feathers. The egg remains there throughout the dark winter days until the chick is born.

Another animal that often stands upright is the meerkat, a kind of mongoose. When out and about with others, one meerkat will stand guard, on the lookout for jackals or eagles.

Many dinosaurs ran about on two feet. One was the tiny hunter *Compsognathus*. It was even shorter than a two-year-old child.

Emperor penguin
4 ft (1.2 m)

48 in (4 ft)

40 in

32 in

Two-year-old child
33 in
(84 cm)

Compsognathus
dinosaur
20 in (50 cm)

Meerkat
12 in (30 cm)

Lesser
mouse deer
8 in (20 cm)
at the
shoulder

in

8
in

0

WITH ITS long neck and legs, the giraffe is the tallest animal in the world. It lives on the grasslands of Africa. Its great height allows it to feed on the leaves and fruits at the very top of the trees. To drink or eat grass, however, a giraffe must spread its legs—or else its head can't make the long journey down to the ground!

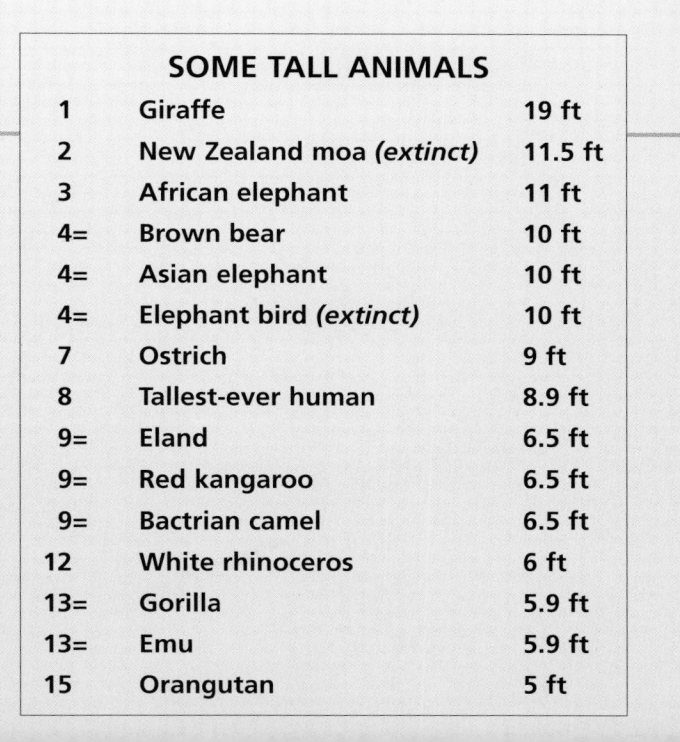

**Giraffe
19 ft (5.7 m)**

Giraffes usually live in family groups of up to 12 animals. To rest, they may lie down for a few hours or sleep standing up.

An angry brown bear standing up on its back legs is only a half the height of a giraffe. But it would still be a frightening sight for a person! Brown bears, including grizzlies, live in northern and mountainous areas of North America, Europe, and Asia. They are meat-eaters, but they also feed on fish, fruits, nuts and insects.

Ostriches are the tallest birds in the world today. It is not long ago that some even taller birds lived. The giant moa of New Zealand and the elephant bird of Madagascar, were both, like the ostrich, unable to fly. They were hunted to extinction in the 18th century. The ostrich uses its long neck and good eyesight to spot danger in the dry plains of Africa where it lives. Its powerful legs allow it to run faster than most of its enemies, reaching speeds of up to 45 mph (72 km/h). It is the fastest creature on two legs.

20 ft

15 ft

SOME TALL ANIMALS

1	Giraffe	19 ft
2	New Zealand moa (extinct)	11.5 ft
3	African elephant	11 ft
4=	Brown bear	10 ft
4=	Asian elephant	10 ft
4=	Elephant bird (extinct)	10 ft
7	Ostrich	9 ft
8	Tallest-ever human	8.9 ft
9=	Eland	6.5 ft
9=	Red kangaroo	6.5 ft
9=	Bactrian camel	6.5 ft
12	White rhinoceros	6 ft
13=	Gorilla	5.9 ft
13=	Emu	5.9 ft
15	Orangutan	5 ft

Brown bear
10 ft (3 m)

Ostrich
9 ft
(2.7 m)

Emperor
penguin
4 ft
(1.2 m)

5 ft

0

17

PROBABLY the largest animal that ever walked on land was the dinosaur *Sauroposeidon*. This plant-eater from the same family as *Brachiosaurus* was 30 times larger than the tallest giraffe. It would have stood about three times its height. It lived near the Gulf of Mexico about 110 million years ago. Had it been alive today, *Sauro-poseidon* would have towered over even a four-story building.

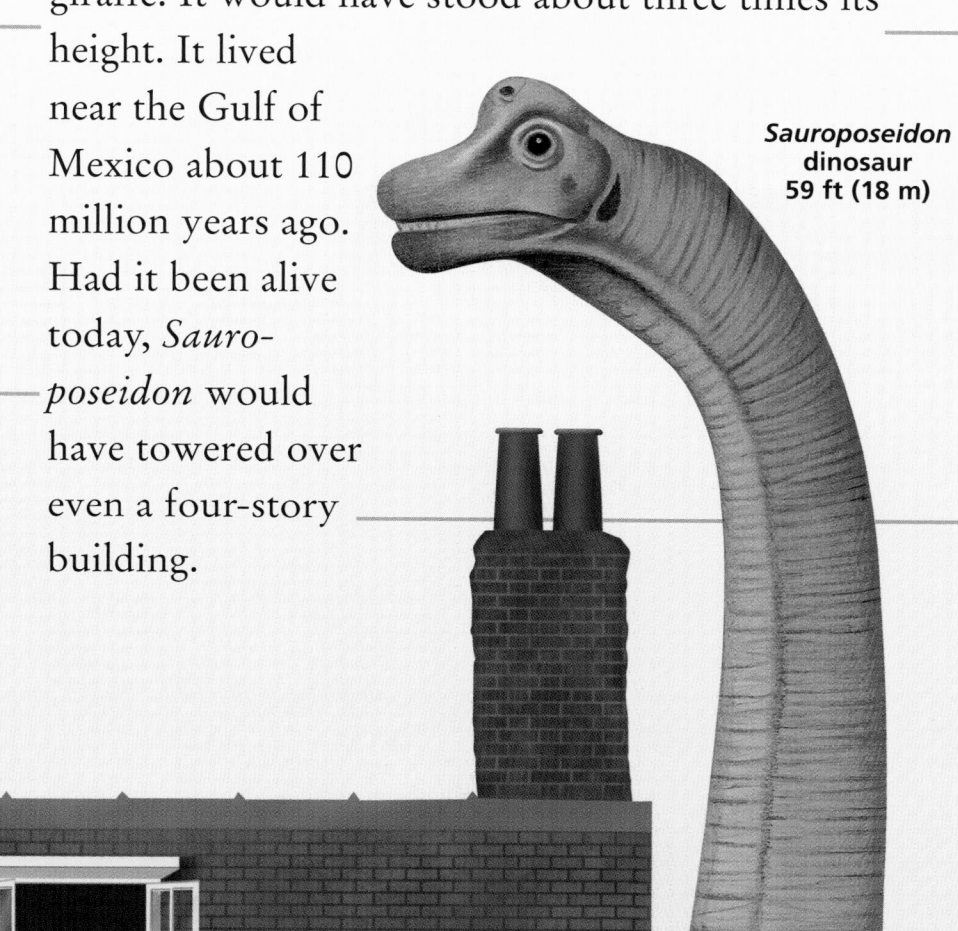

Sauroposeidon dinosaur 59 ft (18 m)

The giant saguaro cactus grows in the Sonoran Desert of southwestern USA and Mexico. There is just enough annual rain for plants to grow in these dry lands. The cactus collects the precious water in its roots then stores it in its thick stem and branches. The saguaro is covered in a waxy layer. This prevents the water from evaporating. The cactus's spines stop animals from eating it. Despite this, the tiny elf owl nests in holes in its stem.

Saguaro cactus 58 ft (17.7 m)

— 60 ft

— 50 ft

— 40 ft

Four-story house 52 ft (16 m)

30 ft

20 ft

Giraffe 19ft (5.7 m)

10 ft

0

19

THE STATUE of Liberty has stood on Bedloe's Island in New York Harbor since 1886. It was one of the first sights seen by millions of people as they came to America from across the sea. The statue has an iron frame on the inside designed by Gustave Eiffel (whose tower is pictured on pages 22-23). A spiral staircase takes visitors up to an observation platform. On the outside, there are about 300 sheets of copper, each about the thickness of a coin.

Another famous, but much older, tower is the Leaning Tower of Pisa in Italy. It started to lean almost as soon as work began on it in 1173. Engineers have recently been able to stop the tower from toppling over by building special supports underneath it.

Just out to sea off some warm coasts, there are great underwater forests. The trees are certain kinds of seaweed called giant kelp. They are anchored to the sea bed by claw-shaped feet, known as holdfasts. Giant kelp can grow at up to 18 inches (45 cm) a day.

THE WORLD'S TALLEST TOWERS

1	CN Tower, Toronto	1,814 ft
2	Ostankino Tower, Moscow	1,761 ft
3	Oriental Pearl Tower, Shanghai	1,535 ft
4	Menara Kuala Lumpur	1,381 ft
5	Central Radio & TV Tower, Beijing	1,368 ft
6	TV Tower, Tianjin	1,361 ft
7	Tashkent Tower	1,230 ft
8	Liberation Tower, Kuwait City	1,214 ft
9	Fernsehturm Tower, Berlin	1,197 ft
10	Stratosphere Tower, Las Vegas	1,148 ft

300 ft

Statue of Liberty 305 ft (93 m)

250 ft

200 ft

Giant kelp 200 ft (60 m)

Leaning Tower of Pisa 180 ft (55 m)

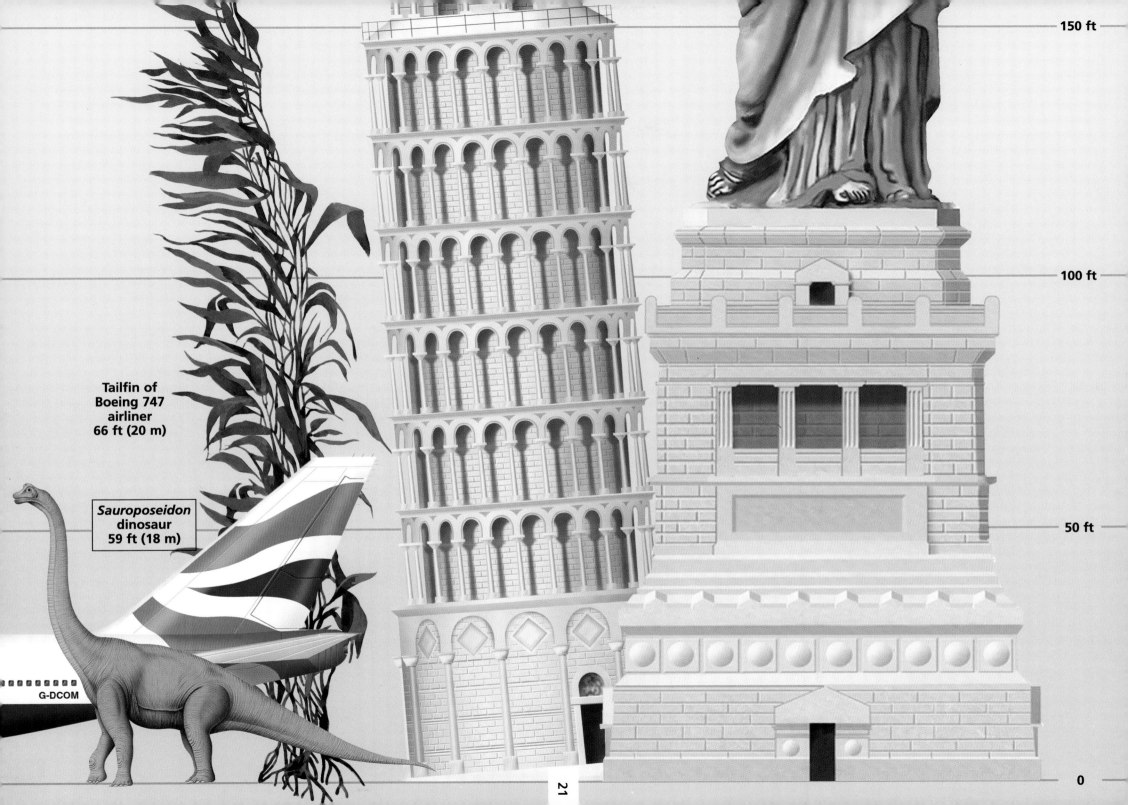

Tailfin of Boeing 747 airliner 66 ft (20 m)

Sauroposeidon dinosaur 59 ft (18 m)

G-DCOM

150 ft

100 ft

50 ft

0

A THE TIME it was completed in 1889, the Eiffel Tower was the tallest structure in the world. It was nearly twice the height of the previous record-holder, the Washington Monument. Built for the Paris Exhibition, the Tower was intended to stand for only 20 years. But it was very popular and has remained standing ever since. Besides offering an incredible view from the top, it has also been used as a weather station and a TV and radio transmitter.

Before the first skyscrapers were built, at the end of the 19th century, churches and cathedrals with tall spires were the world's tallest buildings. The highest spire belongs to the cathedral at Ulm, Germany. Building for the cathedral began in 1377, but it was not finished until more than 500 years later. Modern skyscrapers, like the Bank of China Building, Hong Kong, now tower over the tallest spires.

The Saturn V space rocket, the largest ever built, is as high as a 30-story skyscraper. It launched the Apollo Moon missions in the 1960s and 1970s. The coastal redwood trees, which grow in northern California's coast ranges, are some of the world's tallest trees. Some are about the same height as Saturn V.

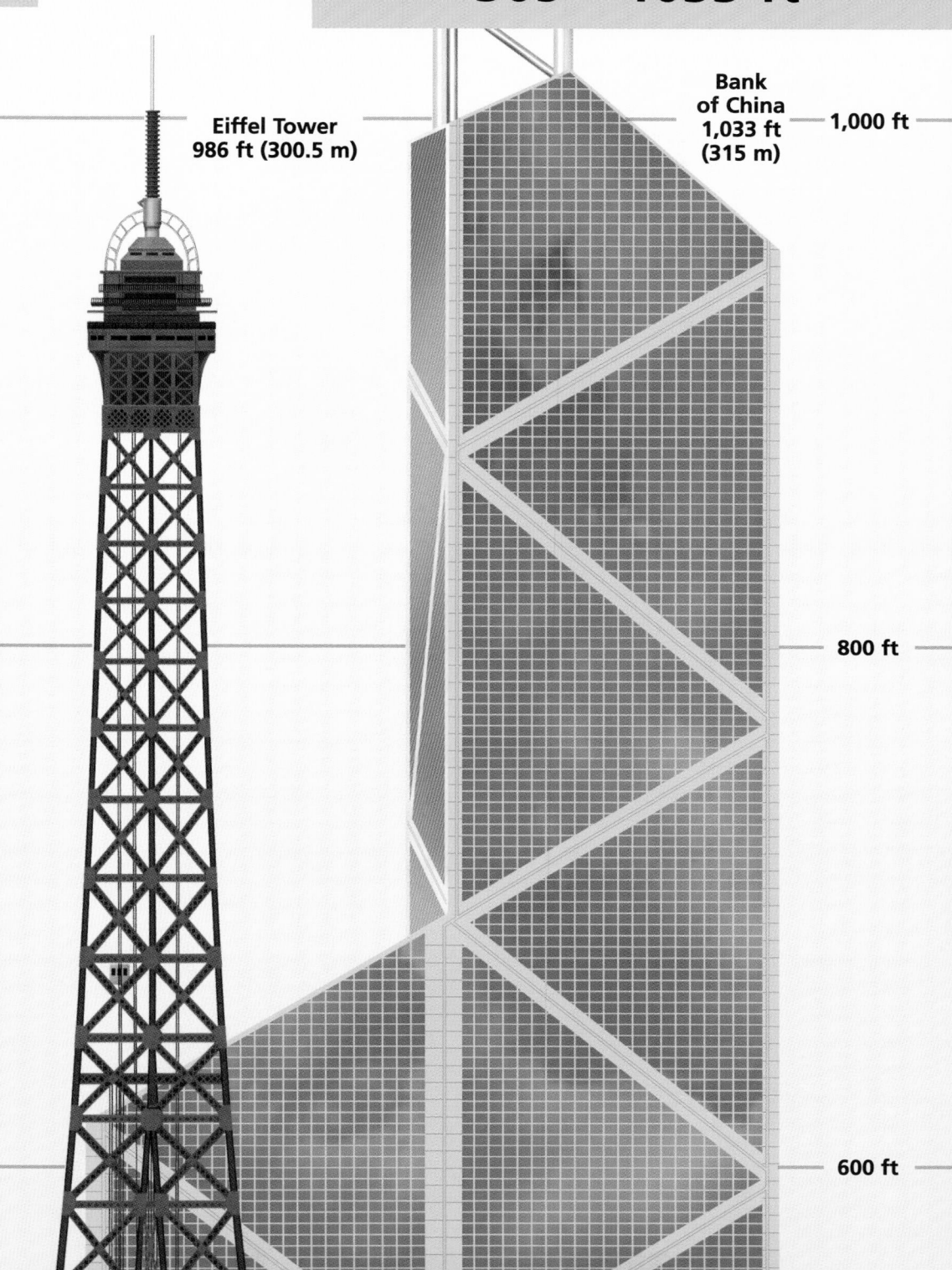

Eiffel Tower
986 ft (300.5 m)

Bank
of China
1,033 ft
(315 m)

1,000 ft

800 ft

600 ft

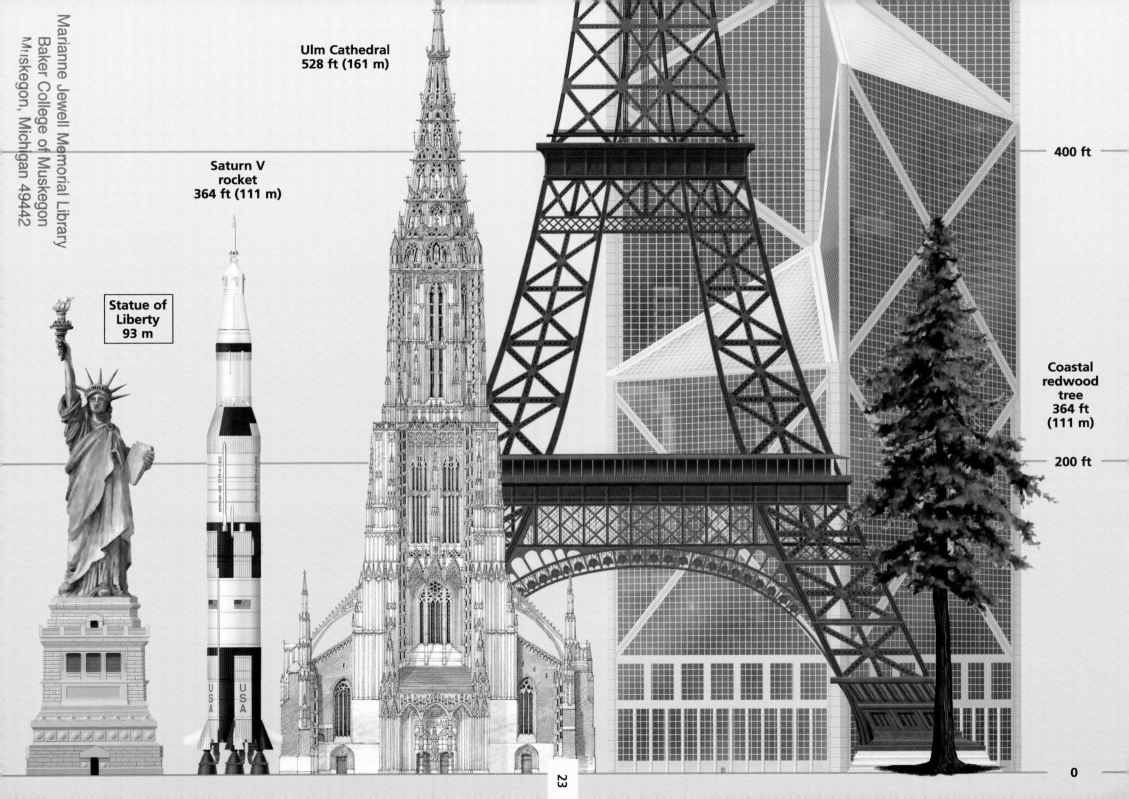

Ulm Cathedral
528 ft (161 m)

Saturn V
rocket
364 ft (111 m)

Statue of
Liberty
93 m

Coastal
redwood
tree
364 ft
(111 m)

400 ft

200 ft

0

SKYSCRAPERS dominate the skyline of many modern large cities in North America and East and Southeast Asia. A skyscraper is a very tall building with a steel frame inside it. Fast elevators take people from ground level to many hundreds of feet up in no time at all.

The Empire State Building is the most famous skyscraper in New York. Completed in only 19 months in 1931, it was the world's tallest building until 1973. The twin Petronas Towers in Kuala Lumpur, Malaysia, hold the record now. These towers are linked by a sky bridge.

The world's tallest unsupported structure is the Canadian National (CN) Tower in Toronto, Canada. It is both a TV transmission station and a tourist attraction. There are two observation decks.

THE WORLD'S TALLEST BUILDINGS

1	Petronas Towers, Kuala Lumpur	1,483 ft
2	Sears Tower, Chicago	1,453 ft
3	Jin Mao Building, Shanghai	1,381 ft
4	Empire State Building, New York*	1,250 ft
5	Central Plaza, Hong Kong	1,227 ft
6	Chicago Beach Tower Hotel, Dubai	1,164 ft
7	Aon Building, Chicago	1,135 ft
8	John Hancock Center, Chicago	1,128 ft

*The twin towers of the World Trade Center in New York City stood at 1,368 ft before they were destroyed in 2001.

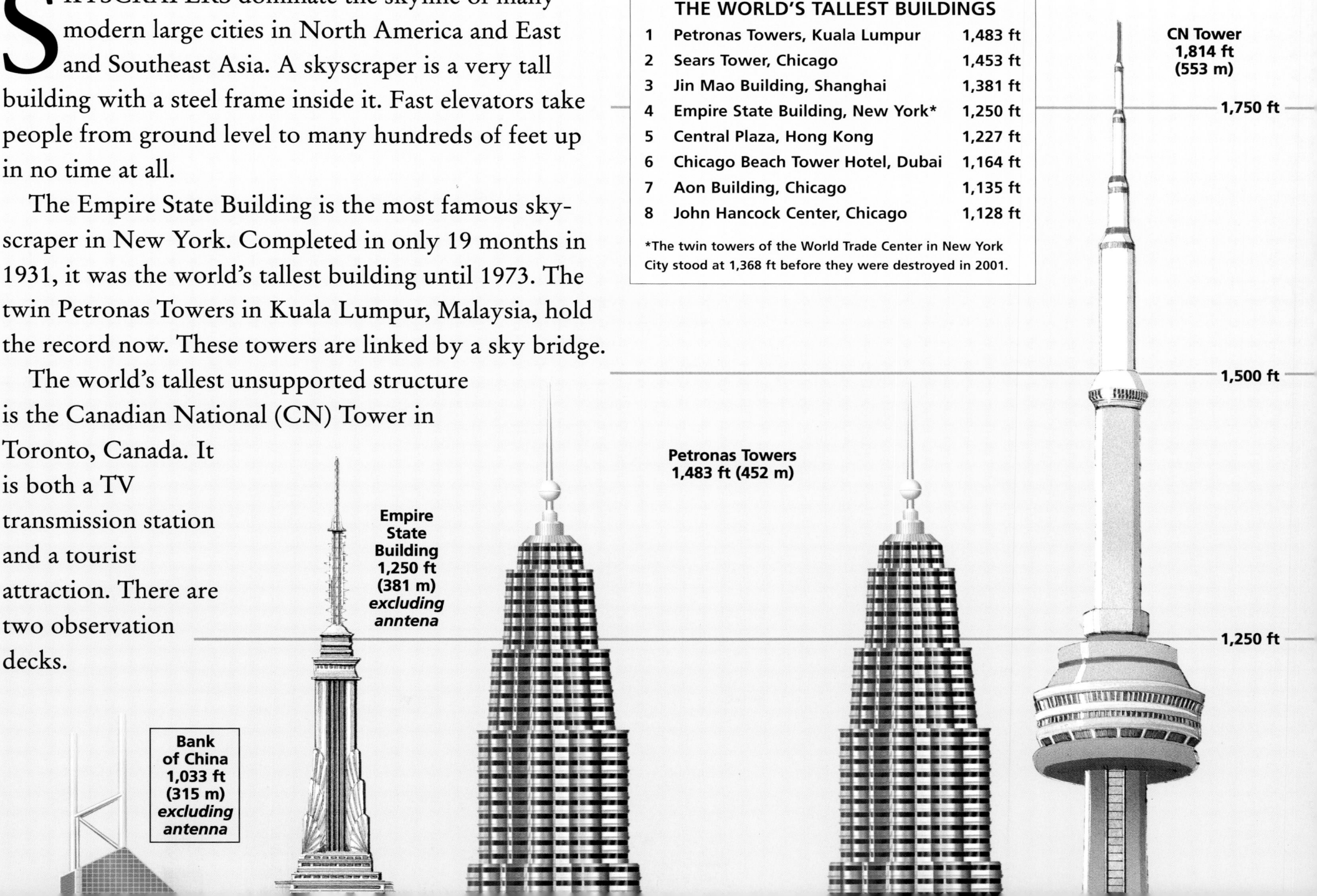

CN Tower
1,814 ft
(553 m)

1,750 ft

Petronas Towers
1,483 ft (452 m)

1,500 ft

Empire State Building
1,250 ft (381 m)
excluding anntena

1,250 ft

Bank of China
1,033 ft (315 m)
excluding antenna

750 ft

500 ft

250 ft

0

**Solar Tower
(2005)
3,280 ft (1000 m)**

**Angel Falls
3,211 ft (979 m)**

ANGEL FALLS in Venezuela, South America, is the highest waterfall in the world. The Carraro River plunges 3,211 feet (979 m) to the rain forest below. For part of the year the water turns to a mist before reaching the bottom. The Falls were named for American pilot Jimmy Angel, who flew his airplane over them in 1935.

Even higher than Angel Falls—and nearly twice as high as the CN Tower—will be the Solar Tower, New South Wales, Australia. Planned for completion in 2005, it will look like a giant chimney. It will produce electricity by sucking in warm air at its bottom through special machines called turbines. It will be surrounded by a circular greenhouse that measures more than 4 miles (7 km) across. Inside, the wind speed will be a steady 34 mph (55 km/h). The tower will be so tall it will be visible 80 miles (130 km) away.

3,000 ft

2,500 ft

2,000 ft

CN Tower
1,814 ft

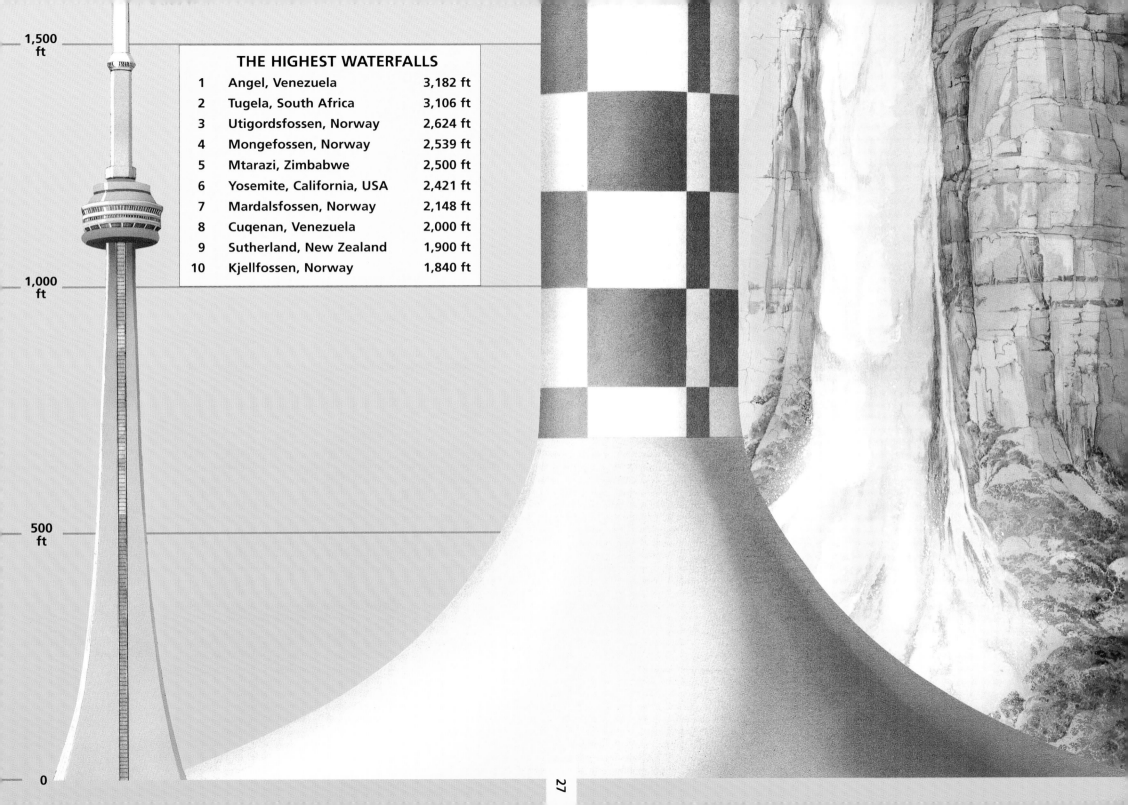

THE HIGHEST WATERFALLS

1	Angel, Venezuela	3,182 ft
2	Tugela, South Africa	3,106 ft
3	Utigordsfossen, Norway	2,624 ft
4	Mongefossen, Norway	2,539 ft
5	Mtarazi, Zimbabwe	2,500 ft
6	Yosemite, California, USA	2,421 ft
7	Mardalsfossen, Norway	2,148 ft
8	Cuqenan, Venezuela	2,000 ft
9	Sutherland, New Zealand	1,900 ft
10	Kjellfossen, Norway	1,840 ft

1,500 ft

1,000 ft

500 ft

0

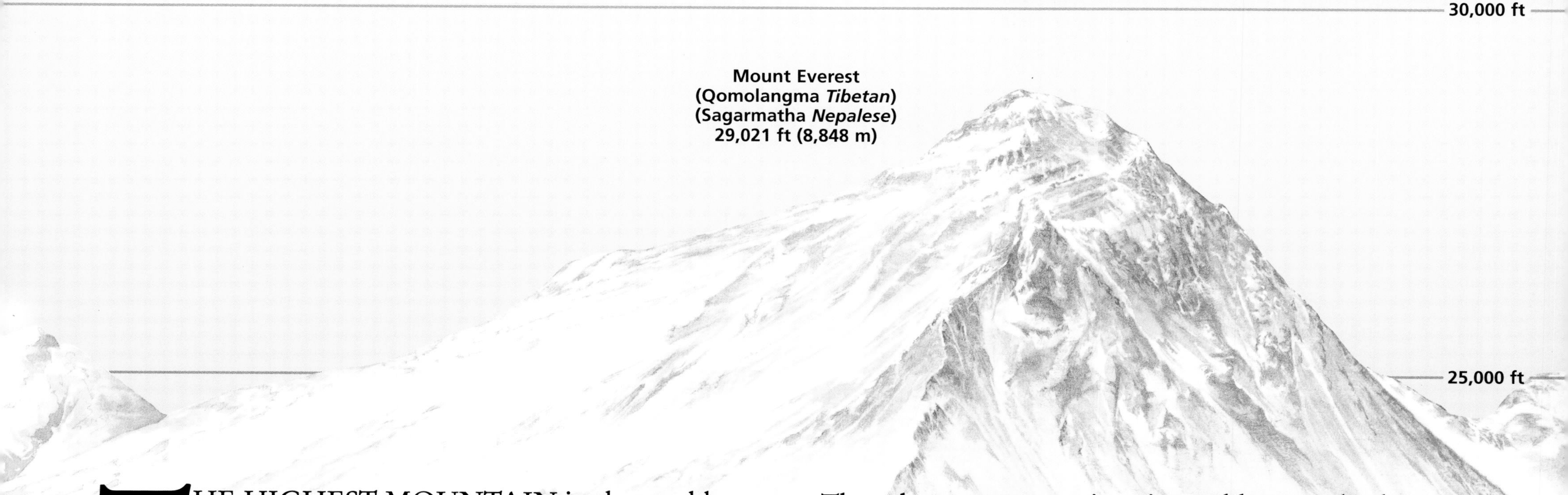

30,000 ft

**Mount Everest
(Qomolangma *Tibetan*)
(Sagarmatha *Nepalese*)
29,021 ft (8,848 m)**

25,000 ft

THE HIGHEST MOUNTAIN in the world, Mount Everest, towers over all the tallest structures ever built. The mountain is located in Asia's Himalaya range. This range forms just part of a long chain of mountains reaching from Europe and the Middle East to Southeast Asia.

The Matterhorn, in the Alps, is another peak in that same mountain chain. Wind, rain, frost and ice all helped to make its jagged shape.

The other two mountains pictured here are both volcanoes. Kilimanjaro is Africa's highest point. Although it lies in the hot tropics, its summit is covered in snow all year round. Vesuvius may have lost more than 6,000 feet (1,900 meters) off its height in the violent eruption of AD 79. The Roman city of Pompeii was destroyed during that eruption.

20,000 ft

**Kilimanjaro
19,339 ft (5,896 m)**

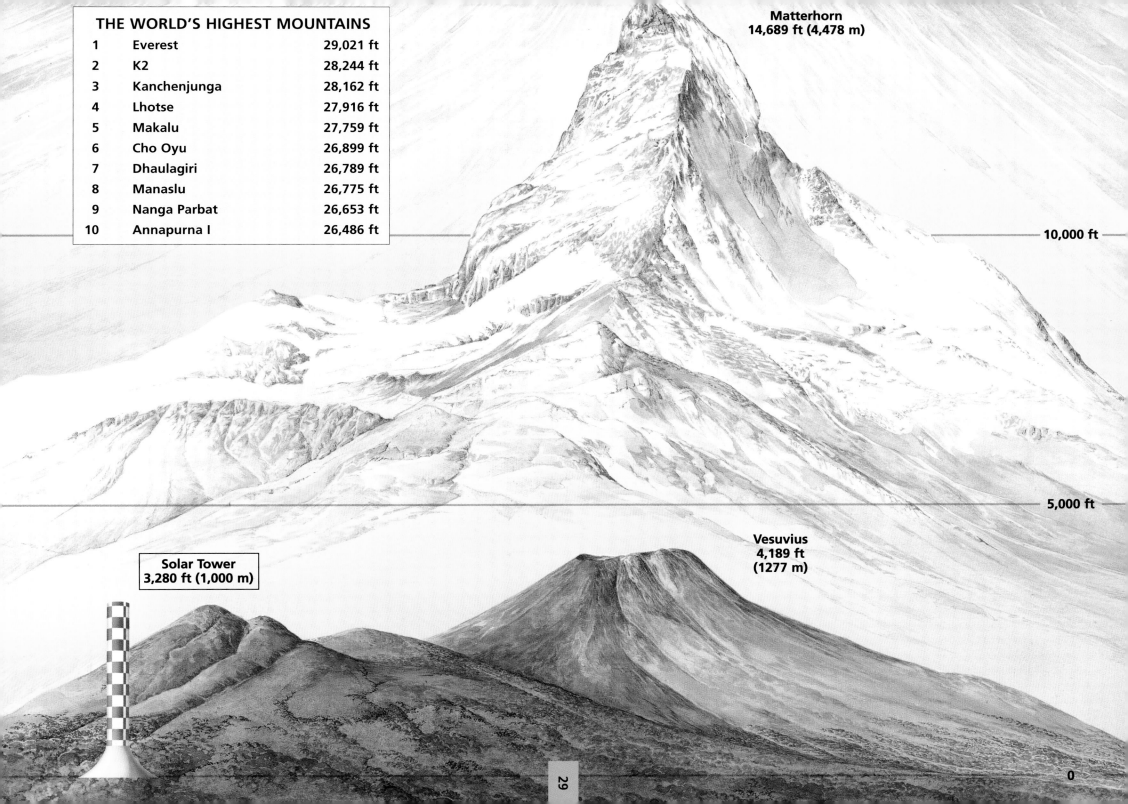

THE WORLD'S HIGHEST MOUNTAINS

1	Everest	29,021 ft
2	K2	28,244 ft
3	Kanchenjunga	28,162 ft
4	Lhotse	27,916 ft
5	Makalu	27,759 ft
6	Cho Oyu	26,899 ft
7	Dhaulagiri	26,789 ft
8	Manaslu	26,775 ft
9	Nanga Parbat	26,653 ft
10	Annapurna I	26,486 ft

Matterhorn
14,689 ft (4,478 m)

10,000 ft

5,000 ft

Vesuvius
4,189 ft
(1277 m)

Solar Tower
3,280 ft (1,000 m)

0

INDEX